Letters from a Wounded Heart

Letters from a Wounded Heart

Reflections to Strengthen and Comfort Your Soul

Gerard F. Baumbach

Paulist Press
New York/Mahwah, New Jersey

Cover design by Cynthia Dunne

Interior illustrations by Catherine Fet

Library of Congress Cataloging-in-Publication Data

Baumbach, Gerard F.
    Letters from a wounded heart : reflections to strengthen and comfort your soul / by Gerard F. Baumbach.
    p. cm.
    ISBN 0-8091-3988-X (alk. paper)
        1. Consolation—Prayer-books and devotions—English. I. Title.

BV4905.2.B29 2000
242´.4—dc21

                                                            00-038568

Published by Paulist Press
997 Macarthur Boulevard
Mahwah, New Jersey 07430

www.paulistpress.com

Printed and bound in the
United States of America

A Note to the Reader

Letters

To seekers everywhere,
        in peace, healing, and joy

A Note to the Reader

One day I began writing a letter to God. Amidst the noise and distraction that seemed to be overtaking my day, I sought the comfort of the all-wise and all-loving Consoler.

So I began to write, prayerfully and poetically. And the more I wrote, the more I found myself exploring dimensions of woundedness in life. These dimensions seemed to capture my waking and breathing and reflecting, and challenged me to live each day to its fullness. They compelled me to express in writing my search for union with the Divine Healer.

The poems offered me prayerful retreat into union with the Divine Presence and promoted a deepening of my relationship with God through the gift of relationships with other seekers. I came to know in new and surprising ways the gentle grasp of the Divine Healer and the touch of God's presence in the eyes, hands and hearts of others—especially at times least expected.

The forty themes that form the framework for this book are aspects of woundedness that were particularly meaningful for me. However, as I wrote, I thought there must be other people whose experiences may be similar to my own. There are probably many more themes that could emerge from your own experience of life, in addition to those that appear here.

Perhaps you may find a mirror image of yourself in some of these themes and words. If so, I hope that you might awaken in joy to divine consolation and healing, particularly through your relationships with others. I trust that you will experience the strengthening of your spirit and comforting of your soul through friendships freely given on the path of divine love.

If your heart is wounded, perhaps something you read here will offer a glimpse of healing love for your life. Perhaps you will see in your own woundedness new ways of relating to other people and to the God who calls and who comes, who relieves and replenishes.

Thank you for joining with me on this walk of the seeker and the searcher. May the Divine Healer be your joy and hope and be as close as all who support you today and every day. And may you be a joyful source of hope and trust for others who risk exploring who they are and who they are becoming.

🖝   🖝   🖝

I wish to offer special thanks to Paulist Press and in particular Maria L. Maggi, managing editor, who envisioned with me possibilities for this project when the idea of publishing these reflections was first proposed. I am truly grateful to her and to all who handled with such professional care the preparation and design of the final work.

Letter One: **Woundedness**

Divine Heart,

I am in pain today. I suffer the loss of relationships and wonder how such interior pain can be so deep. Why such solitude? Why such loneliness—is this different, after all, from being alone? in this time and place?

Loving God, thank you for making my woundedness your own.

lonely heart, lonely one
woundedness riding the surf of oceans deep
gently cresting
meandering toward shore
rushing waters embrace the sands
washing them clean

water drifts and cleanses hurts
sands swallow
all that
exposes me

pain now relieved
and joy recovered
but a different joy, O Great Spirit,
one that sees with new eyes
familiar sights and memories long forgotten

pain and joy?
conflict? contradiction?
how, O God?
why, O God?
the cross, the cross...

woundedness healed and life renewed
through sands washed and slowly sifted
by hands you give to hold and heal me
in moments of woundedness

Letter Two: **Relationship Healing**

Divine Heart,

My mind races away sometimes, my lips spill over with fumbled words whose meanings only you know. Yet I know you come to me in relationships least expected. Is this how you came to your first disciples? Were they acquaintances, friends, relatives (You know, Lord, we do not get to pick our family!)?

Healing Lord, make my gratitude cover my love for you as I bring joy to all you give me to love.

thoughts of life
unsettled, unfulfilled
so many worries
on which to focus

but you surprise me
in my search for healing in my life

I become
your healer

yes, me!
to my sister, my brother
made one in you

how can I search with them?
what if they walk too fast?
or too slow?

God, I am not able, I say
I am not stable, I pray
but you know for ever
your will
your call
your love

in the healing sought
your healing love is found
in others

your healing announced
through fumbled words
and flickering faith
of a wounded poet

Letter Three: **Openness to Others**

Great Comforter,

Lives cross as people do at a congested intersection. I twist, I turn, I try to avoid colliding with others, sometimes failing and sometimes succeeding. Oh, I see the other side of the street, but the getting there is so often fraught with danger, or at least a little bit of risk. Is it always better to avoid the collision, Lord? Who do you give me to guide me, to take my hand and lead the way? How do you come to me today?

Lord, make my heart rest in you as I see your love in my beloved companions on your way. Might I hear more clearly now words old yet ever new, "Come, follow me!" Let me be open—truly open—to all whom you send me. They are your healers, too.

windy and cold
the breeze chills the soul
I await these few hours
a time to unfold

I fear being open
I fear what might flow
yet hearts ache with truth
to whom shall I go?

be with me for ever
in smile and in song
be present in Spirit
in you all life long

oh wonder of all love
oh comfort so near
hold my heart in you
relieve all my fear

for time is not mine
as only you know
you ask me to stop
and pause so to grow

such is the struggle
that peers through the dawn
just know I still need you
in eve and in morn

Letter Four: **Incompleteness**

Source of All Goodness,

I scan the horizon of my life, sometimes straining to see the wonders you have created. In my fleeting glance I see many things and sometimes look—yes, perhaps even with envy—at others' seeming happiness and wonder where I went wrong. Why, I ask myself, do I sense I am not whole? How incomplete I feel today!

Lord, help me to know that I am your blessing. In others' abundant love may I grasp your eternal love and, with your grace, testify of your wonders, now and for ever.

another approaches
and another
one more

crossing my path
causing me
to question, to wonder

oh, Lord,
who are they?
why my path?
why today?

life incomplete
spirit needing more
I seek not another
to open your door

but gently you move me
to see
in sisters and brothers
what your presence can be

completeness residing
not only in one
but in another and one more

you come, O Christ,
in paths crossed
and lives mixed

treasured moments
of completeness

Letter Five: **Water**

Divine Provider,

The earth you give yields fruit to see and touch, to smell and taste, to refresh and strengthen. Earthen soil yearns for seeds to take root and slowly grow, watered by the symbol so central to our baptism.

I am one of your seeds, Lord. What saturates my life, my home, my relationships? What goes unsatisfied for lack of my sensing your nurturing my life?

Loving God, continue to water me with the witness of your people.

saturated, soaked
emerging
from waters
that contain me no more

hands outstretched
grasping
reaching
not letting go

momentarily
I resist
fearing the touch
the newness
the stranger

but in the emergence
from waters deep
calm overcomes me
it is you, Lord,
who lifts me up

safe in your abundant embrace
I glisten
through the wetness
of grace offered
by wet and sacred hands

baptism freshness renewed
through hands outstretched
graced hands
hands of life
hands divine

Letter Six: *Absence*

Present and Holy One,

Where are you, Lord? Why do I search? Why can I not see you before me? I need you now, Lord, here, Lord!

But, wait...I see one before me...I don't expect this one to be the one to mirror for me your grace, your presence, your love. Oh, God, not that person! But stillness overcomes me, and I cannot contain my love for you...I must approach the unnamed one before me who is not just approaching but reaching out to *me*. Oh, God, I am not ready...is my sense of your being absent from me really my lack of awareness of your approaching me in the unexpected?

Lord of absence, move me to fill others' aches of absence with the witness of your love burning in my heart.

void
empty
barren
hollow

dry
lonely
weary
my desert heart

thirsting for you, Lord,
yearning for presence past
in the present

not a mirage of love, of hope
but the abode
of eternal truth
and love found

even in desert sands
now swirling
Spirit breeze and Spirit breath

windmakers we become
the witness of a people
in shifting sands
your holy presence
absence no more!

Letter Seven: **Body Broken**

Divine Creator,

Years come, years go. My mind stays sharp, my ideas as fresh as ever. Yet the body in which they dwell challenges my spirit. My body feels broken, health escaping daily. I become irritated sometimes, frustrated over illness, pain, lingering concerns for body health.

But is it body health, my Creator? Or is it rather whole health? Am I not a whole person made in your image and likeness? So when my body aches, all of who I am is challenged. And I sense a change in others, too. Though my physical malady resides only in me, symptoms seem to appear in those around me as well. Again, the lesson: We are one.

Lord, my spirit struggles to soar in such moments. Be with me, still my pain, let me see your presence in the kind touch and healing hearts of those you give as gift to me. Empower me, Loving Creator, to link my suffering with that of others, and together, to that of your Son.

what?
a spot?
an unclear test?

why?
why me?
why us?

what is normal, Lord?
who is normal, Lord?

God of my questioning
be with me
in moments uncertain
moments given
in fullness of life

actions forgiven
hurts softened

hearts healed
beating together
a symphony
of endless wonder
moving for ever
your people
healed as one
in you

Letter Eight: **Vocation**

God of the Plan,

The signs point, but I still seem directionless. Clarity escapes me when I get close to what I believe is your will. As I seek and search, things begin to come into focus...but then, like a song ending, clarity slowly drifts away.

What is your song for my life, O God? How do I come to know your will? Whom do you offer to help me see what I am called by you to be and to do?

Lord of all vocation, guide me in your way. Help me see all the paths you offer me to travel...paths of life linked for ever to your Son. Give me the grace of your Spirit to choose wisely and to listen attentively to your voice...gently calling, softly leading, always loving.

children's dreams
stay with me
secure in future thoughts
I see

yet soon you come
ways strange and real
freedom calling
through dreams ideal

decisions galore
grasp my soul

how to love you, Lord?
how to serve?
do I have the will?
the nerve?

you probe my soul
your servants lead
what am I to do?
I plead
for future thoughts
are now, I see

friends come forth
sense my fright
take my hand
your new light

Letter Nine: **Misunderstanding**

God of Clarity,

It was clear to *me*. I waited all week for the meeting. Everything was in order. This time I really tried to "get it right." So what happened, Lord? Before I knew it, a relationship was upset, unfortunate comments made, leaving me feeling weakened, humiliated and needing to start over again. Why can't this person see as clearly as I do?

In the moment of my self-questioning, you came, Lord...asking *me* to see more clearly! What? I thought I already knew the answer to the situation at hand...everything was in order...but now you probe more deeply, leading me to hear the other with ears opened and released from the silence of the self.

extra hours, extra days
time escapes my grasp
in the getting ready
the preparation
the perfection of my effort

the need to please
envelops me
consumes me
as I seek to defeat
misunderstanding

but alas!
surface talk reveals confusion
how? why?
I worked so long, so hard!

in the gulf between words spoken not heard
your probing presence gradually
warms my ears
a new vision before me
yielding understanding

your clarity
comes as a bridge
linking people
joining thoughts, then words
finally understanding

Letter Ten: **Unwelcome Quiet**

God of Joyful Noise,

I used to wonder about all the noise! People coming and going, children happily declaring "their home" as the neighborhood center. Those days, long past but not forgotten, remind me of your presence in the vitality and robust movement of the people-blessings in my life.

But now they are gone. I weary of the quiet that now is the strongest noise. It seems so peaceful that the silence comes as a deafening roar! Though lives have moved on, the spirit of blessing remains, not as some nostalgic moment, but in the aromas, the marks, the treasures of a lifetime of blessing in the noise.

Lord of Joyful Noise, be always present to me in the sounds, the memories, the silences of life.

turn down the TV!
quiet that stereo!
wow! great! super!

and suddenly they are gone
at least face-to-face
not the constructed noises
but the human voices
of laughter, joy
sorrow, calm

still I hear them
such familiar reassurance

in the quiet of the moment
I reach out
grasp the quiet
no longer unwelcome
and hear the noise
of presence past

the mystery of your presence
given in noisy lives
now distant in space
and present in thundering silence
in my days, my nights

Letter Eleven: *Tears*

God of the Rainfall,

My eyes turn moist, dampened by a thought, a word, a touch. I can be rejoicing at the birth of a child, sharing the pain of a dear friend who is ill beyond hope of recovery, viewing a moving drama on television or simply reflecting on a life lived fully yet incompletely.

Cry? Me? People would be surprised, wouldn't they? Yet so much of my body is moisture anyway, that it is no less than natural to allow my eyes to become conduits of deep joy...compassion...sadness...strength. In the droplets called tears, somehow I come to see through cloudy eyes ever more clearly your call and your people.

Lord, make the mists that shape and color my vision into emblems of immersion in your life.

my tears
swell the sight of life
and cloud the vision of the present

memories of other days
evoked, brought forward
some happier now than before
others simply clouded

my being drained
of
securities deeply anchored
tempting thoughts of emptiness and fear

my tears
dried by hands
reaching through foggy mists
cleansing me from inner pain
of
dreams shattered, hopes vanished

human strength now preserved
every glance wet with joy
happiness resurfacing
another witness
emerging
absorbing my tears

Letter Twelve: **Indifference**

Wisdom of the "Unimportant Ones,"

You know me, Lord. I am a ho-hum person, somehow blending into the woodwork during an office meeting or fading into the scenery at a social event. People struggle to remember my name: "What did you say you do, anyway?" (As if who I am and my worth are defined by what I do all day!)

Yes, Lord, you know me in moments when I feel ignored and simply unimportant. In these moments I am the "average" person—viewed by some as a bland Jane or John Doe, living a routine life and enjoying neither great success nor prominent failure—certainly not a headline grabber!

Be with me, O Spirit of God, and ignite the gifts of your presence in me as I offer my simple ways of life, love, and hope to others in the numerous opportunities before me each day.

ho-hum
no matter
so what
no difference made anyway

empty impressions
erroneous signs of
disinterest
unimportance

am I just another
person of the universe?
a nameless nobody?

never!

I am yours, O Wisdom,
greatly treasured
given to others
to share
gifts of faith
given

to be your light
your wisdom
your voice
the unsung ho-hum
becoming hallelujah!

Letter Thirteen: **Prophet without Honor**

Forgotten Lord,

How odd it seems that loyal work turns to tarnished value for "services rendered." The "last one in the door" bears the favored message; the one with years of solid service "lacks" credibility and wisdom—despite on-the-scene experience.

Lord, many did not see your wisdom, your gift of self to a people crying out. You were put to the test many times, but remained one for all people, though without honor.

Cradle me with your love, Lord, uniting me to you in a prophetic and honorable embrace. I know you value—through the affirmation of your people—my gift of work to the world around me.

ideas, dreams, plans
better ways
brought forward

suggestion boxes
weary from touch

ideas, dreams, plans
unopened
unread

other hands
pass by
passive ignorance
the seeming value

then the box cries out!
note the note
of the faithful servant!

one's
ideas, dreams, plans
gain life
embraced by all

an honorable
witness
shaping
community's
ideas, dreams, plans

Letter Fourteen: **Naïveté**

God of Innocence,

Sails swing in the wind, moving the vessel of my life here, there and everywhere. I seem to shift from place to place, side to side, front to back, not knowing—only sensing—the intensity of movement beneath the choppy surface.

Oh, but once in a great while I sense something more...that I am out of the loop, missing the point, just sailing along with little awareness of what others take for granted. I am, as they say, "a bit naïve."

Sometimes new awareness may even bring new pain. Yet my naïve spirit is trusting, harmless, childlike, rich in compassion and lost in love. Thank you, God of Innocence, for the gift of gentleness in people who permit me no regrets when I do not miss what I am missing.

thoughts swirling
wonder stretching
spirit soaring
of such simple beauty
is the innocent self

others
"in the know"
believe me silly
in my unknowing
ways

other others
see through eyes now clear
of savvy ways
ways proven true
ways speaking
redemption

through
others' eyes
and ways
your way, your people
become one within
innocence

unchained love
coaxed to surface
reality

Letter Fifteen: **Death**

God of Eternal Rest,

Tell me why...please! Why this loss? Don't you know my need? The unspeakable pain? The grief, the silence, the emptiness within? I wonder if anything can ever heal the woundedness I am feeling. Who will take the place of my beloved?

I am tempted to resist resting in you, my God, even as my beloved now rests in the garden of new life. Why can't your harvest time spring forth when I decide that I am really ready?

I can't believe I am thinking this way. I am just hurting, Lord. Death makes me all mixed up. Yes, you know the unspeakable pain, the loss. Yet you continue to immerse me in the power of your eternal embrace. Please, God, never let go.

good-bye wave
final kiss
weakened grip

fading whispers
delicate breaths
change overcoming
the beloved one

movement to eternity
so hard, so very hard
for a wounded survivor

lingering loss
images from the past
treasured reminders
of beloved presence

death's claim
of absence asserted
now overcome

mysterious glimpses
of time transformed
the embrace of grace
clothing all your beloved
in faith hope love

change overcoming me

Letter Sixteen: **Spirit-Hunger**

God of Healing,

"Fast life, fast food, ready to serve, reheat. Follow the directions on the side of the box, then dispose of the heating container in an environmentally safe way. Ahh...hunger satisfied."

Is this the meal I yearn to share, Lord? Or does something else take hold, propelling me to seek relief for hungers of restlessness, woundedness, yearning—hungers satisfied neither simply nor alone?

Be with me, Lord, as I attend to hungers seen through images of others' yearnings, reminding me of our deep and lasting communion in you.

hungers hidden
swirling deep
inside

the outside image
the story of a face
surface glow of peace
impressions of pain no more
joy for sure

still you hear
cries for release
a restless spirit
reaching out, reaching far
searching high, searching low

then I see
others seem like me
hearts bursting
hungers craving relief

yearnings
needs pains joys
come together
your love unleashed

one hope in healing
gently softly mercifully
your communion
restlessness no more

Letter Seventeen: **Armchair Energy**

God of the Weary,

I am tired. I am *very* tired. Work all day, sleep...some nights. Sometimes others tell me that I behave as if I believe that my mandate is to "do it all." I just feel so overwhelmed by what I am supposed to do and the expectations that others have of me (or so I surmise).

When I do get a break, I position myself comfortably in a favorite chair and then fall asleep! Somehow I feel as if I am on an endless cycle, existing on armchair energy day after day. I am even afraid that any change might knock me off the cycle...then what?

Lord of the Weary, give me hands to grasp as I risk leaping from the wheel of weariness to seeking with others a life of balance in endless witness to your love.

quick!

e-mail sending
beeper signaling
cell phone ringing
train creeping
traffic converging

when, O God, will it stop?
when, O God, will I stop?

energy spent
messages sent
travel and task
no hour the last

through a wilderness
of weariness
tired eyes awaken to
soul refreshers

witnesses of balance
surrounding me
people practical
ideal and real

gentle spirits
blending task and rest
offering glimpses
of life in the balance

Letter Eighteen: *Generation* ____

God without Labels,

How attractive it becomes to tackle the problems of the generations by labeling those more energetic but perhaps less wise than "older folk," Generation ___. You see, Lord, I cannot even write or say the common label. How can I assign your younger blessings such a judgmental label? If they are "Generation ___," then how might I label my own generation?

Lord, I ponder what my generation—and those of my ancestors—are handing on to the ones identified by the mark of a wrong answer. Sadly, I cannot help but think that the record of the generations of the twentieth century passed to the youth who lead the charge into the future is tarnished by scenes of inhumanity, violence, weariness and distance. Is this their inheritance?

Make the scales fall from my eyes as I gaze upon today's lowly ones. Guide me, Lord, to reserve judgment when I see a younger person who is not just like me.

new people
emerging, energetic
attitudes
language
messages
foreign to an aging ear

wisdom ignored
experience questioned
how dare they!

don't they know
who I am?

aha! insight!
is this all about me?
Or...you?

do you really expect me
to see you
in
baggy pants?
in
questioning voices?

oh, how I need my brothers and sisters
to help me to see you
in my brothers and sisters

Letter Nineteen: *Saying Good-Bye*

God beyond Farewells,

She has to go. He won't be back for awhile. They're moving clear across the country!

How quickly words fade into whispers as I offer good-byes to friends and family members. Some occasions warrant simple messages delivered by a glance, while others yearn for more. It's always hard to say good-bye, but never hard to live in the memory of friendships cherished and persons present in fading whispers.

God beyond Farewells, be with my friends, family and me in the going and the staying. And fill the space and time between with the whispering presence of your Spirit.

whispering voices
drifting away
soundings
now afterglow

seclusion emerging
presence fading
assurances of communion
demanding reassurance

farewells center stage
disappearing images
blending
into horizons of good-bye

though fields of farewells
absorb my thirsty self
whispering breath surfaces

hearing wounded eyes
anonymous comforters
reclaim my spirit
brightening horizons

your messengers
easing good-byes
mingling spirits
healing in the seeing

Letter Twenty: **Compromise**

Gentle Father,

"My way is just fine, thank you. I've thought it out and decided the best way to proceed. Oh, you want to talk about it? Well, I don't think that's really necessary...."

Sometimes I see the "wisdom" of my insights so clearly that no other approach could possibly be more effective. Hah! Who am I kidding?

Kind and gentle Father, remind me to pause, to see another way, to compromise with others today.

shears of confidence
prune away others' ideas
snippets float toward the ground,
roots of solitary planting still in place

ideas of a single sower
dominate and direct
plans for the way
no other seeds welcome today

my vision of progress
shared by just me
why don't others
see what I see?

compromise, compromise!
I seem now to hear
your will clearly present
in gentle people's ideas

wise counsel of others
shared vision and hope
moves my surrender
unmasks covers of fear

how rich the planting
with seeds of ideas
blended as one
for a moment at least

Letter Twenty-one: **Injustice**

Just and Holy One,

It sure seems odd to me that the word *just* is so often connected to the word *war.* Yet the same adjective is essential for probing the mystery of your eternal presence, Just and Holy God.

Do I really look beyond color, creed, ethnic identity or cultural heritage in dealing with others? "What can I do?" I plead, as my thoughts turn to suffering continents worlds away...and then back again to lands and hands close by.

Loving God, help me rid myself of whatever might prevent me from working with others to overcome systems that deny the dignity and beauty of life—your gift to every person.

upward economy
markets galore
poverty silenced?
eco-pain no more?

needs beyond
plate and place
needs beyond
financial chase

energies spent
your poor reach out
sisters and brothers
eagerly shout

"we are hungry for justice!
are we not all your poor?
these wounded dry hands
must suffer no more!"

yielding to love
mixed faces step forth
wounded surroundings
rise and now shout

"sing songs of justice!
proclaim hope galore
system changers and savers
mute spirits no more!"

Letter Twenty-two: **Environment**

Lord of the Land,

Is it possible for life to become litter? What a terrible thought! So forgive me, Lord, and let me explain.

Papers cling to fences, lay curbside on a street or float aimlessly through the air. I wonder about the trees of life from which society's newest waste takes shape. The same emotion surfaces as instant images of global destruction flash before my eyes, revealing a pained earth in need of healing, a world weary from intentional destruction of your gift of life in the land.

Why does human life treat nonhuman life so indiscriminately? Lord, be the gardener of my spirit. Guide my decision making so I will be ever mindful of nonhuman living things and their origin in you, the tree of life.

third day of creation
crying out
wanton woundedness
suffering of another sort

ravaged lands
fields, flowers
forests, waters
defenseless

global evidence
conviction enough
tombs of litter
raise creation's question:

why trample underfoot?

lands one
as are peoples
hearts and soil softening
common blending

burst of beauty
reckless disregard no longer
earth's celebration
stewards of the third day
now rejoicing

Letter Twenty-three: **Impatience**

Benefit of the Wait,

Seconds, minutes, hours become days, weeks, years. Decisions only dreamed about are delayed again, unable to come to life. Impatience becomes my lifestyle.

I've waited long enough, Lord. I know what I want. The struggles you experienced in hoping your disciples would understand you demanded great patience, I am sure, but I struggle to model my waiting on yours. I want certain things to happen now! Is that too much to ask (respectfully, of course!)? I just don't have the time.

Christ, Benefit of all who wait, calm me. Thank you for friends who help me to take a deep breath as I work my way through life's daily agenda.

rush
becomes me
sweeping hand
the hand that guides

glow-in-the-dark movement
controls my way
too slow again
today

who has time
to pause? to breathe?
please, God, more time!

your invitation
divine offering
advent moment
perspective time

patient hands
form an arc of love

in a waiting gesture
and sweeping embrace
calm surrounds me

in the breathing
the greater benefit
impatience now
only a matter of time

Letter Twenty-four: **One Step Behind**

Loving Companion,

You can pick me out, Lord. A conversation moves ahead rapidly. I watch as others complete page two while I am still scanning headlines on page one. I am stepping up to the table for an appetizer while others are finishing a main course. I am a step behind...or so it looks.

If truth be told, I travel the way of faith with the gifts and abilities given me in love by you. There is no front or back, right or left, top or bottom, ahead or behind to your love. You freely offer me depths of love in endless measure, love so vast that horizons fade into infinity.

Come, Lord Jesus. Be with me when I appear to be one step behind, but am really in step with you.

distance lengthened
limits stretched
seeming judgment:
pace too slow

I look around
suppressing views
that being first
still makes the news

look again
I hear you say
people paths
your walking way

sacred walk
no steps behind
in your walk
converging minds

common steps
eternal glimpse
walking witness
life eclipsed

ahead, behind
now no more
people paths
horizon's door

Letter Twenty-five: **Loss of Memory**

Keeper of All Memories,

Simple things. Keys, papers, books. Items misplaced more than really forgotten. But sometimes I wonder about my ability to recall events, persons or things. Lord, I am told that at my age this is nothing to be alarmed about, but, you see, I have witnessed memory loss up close.

When Dad became ill and was unable to recall how to perform even the simplest of tasks, Mom became his living memory. Their children joined her in becoming not just memory makers but memory keepers, guardians of one simple life. Treasures once forgotten became priceless gems to be handed on to new generations.

Eternal Guardian, preserve within me life's yesterdays.

eyes once crisp
storied record
vigor and life
now hidden

family history
his story, her story
swallowed up
mental resistance weakening

scrambled words
blurred tones
all that remains
of memory shattered

so many memories
fading fast
with, within
my beloved

in a whispering glance
you appear
to memory keepers
through storied eyes

family preservers
your inspiration
memory's guardians
death's pending claim defeated
memory victorious

Letter Twenty-six: **Chaos**

Conqueror of Chaos,

This time I thought I had it all together. But, alas, I ended up all over the place! I used to have everything in order. Friends' musings served as gentle reminders that I could organize anything. But now all that is awry. Why?

My head spins in a whirling mixture of responsibilities and distractions, preventing me from getting "really important" things done. I am pulled in many directions; chaos surrounds me.

Creator God, thank you for all who are order restorers in my life. They calm me.

downward spiral upward
forward movement in retreat
curves looking straight
in a world spinning erratically

tumult
becomes me
as inner tornadoes
swirl randomly

exhaustion demands
my spirit rest
in the midst of
everything nowhere
nothing everywhere

chaos acting the victor
sees not the swells
of inner peace
arising

carriers of calm
couriers of form
sisters and brothers
images and likenesses

your vehicle
healing a spiritual void
formlessness no more

chaos to calm
you come, Lord

Letter Twenty-seven: **Noise Pollution**

Lord of Quiet,

Trains, screeching vehicles, planes overhead, the whir of highway traffic, wailing sirens—a wild assembly of noise acts not in concert but in random disarray. Debilitating noise pollutes my soul and pains my ears.

I yearn for quiet, which I think all too quickly to be the opposite of noise. Then I realize that tranquil sound is the nemesis of noise pollution. I hear it in places real and imagined—running brooks, wind rushing by, familiar voices of love. I call such tranquility quiet, but you know what I mean.

Lord of Quiet, help me in aiding others to know your tranquil presence in the sounds of every day.

what?
I can't hear!
oh, that's what you said!
of course, if I heard you right!

pounding sounds
stun sensibilities and
reverberate invisibly
straining cushions in my head

waves of resonance
in irregular movement
gain volume and
implode inside me

head soundproofing only a start
internal alarms sound the alert
to seek not just ear cover
but sources that steal the stilled moment

why my surprise
when I see
people like me
seeking your peace

frantic fulminations now gone,
I see in other voices your quiet
and hear in their eyes a
common need in uncommon noise

Letter Twenty-eight: *Parched Land*

Father and Creator,

Blessed and helpless at the same time. That's how I feel, Lord. You entrust to me and to my sisters and brothers your gift of the land on which we live. But how are we, how am I, to practice stewardship when our gift is dry? when the rains do not come?

Drought narrows my focus, making me think almost exclusively of caring for *my* land: my lawn, my plants, my garden. How silly this is. In my struggle to understand private ownership of land as a temporary state of affairs, I finally realize that you hold the eternal deed, Lord.

Caring Creator, inspire me to join with others in seeking ways of relieving Earth's drought. Help me to realize that, while people need water nourishment, your land does, too.

oh, cherished earth!

moans of parched land
echo through choking dust

leaves separate from limbs
in search of a sip of your watering gift

drooping branches
fall weakly below

wildflowers hang uniformly
too weak to swing in a welcome breeze

parched land a reminder to people worldwide:

be one together
forget all your pride
drought has no favorites
no preference or side

Creator of all
our watering plea
open your clouds and send springs of life
make of us
watering witnesses
as your world spins athirst

Letter Twenty-nine: **Bad News**

Nurturing Spirit of God,

Some days I seem to convince myself that living the good news means living in the absence of bad news. What happens to the way I live the good news when I receive bad news? Or when I am the bearer of bad news?

The lessons of life teach me that bad news comes in the midst of living a life formed by the good news of Jesus Christ.

Be with me, O Spirit of God. Give me the gift of perspective when bad news and I get together. Through the goodness of others, nurture and guide me in the use of your gifts, especially when I find myself dealing with bad news.

a good start!
at work on time today
ready for the influx
plans, papers, people

my open door
swings silent
no disturbance for now
so I do what I need to do

then a series of rings
silence interrupted
now becoming a moment
of summoning diversion

what? when?
what? no!
bad news strikes
no notice, only shock

life needs surface
beyond plans and papers
my need for you suddenly present
bad news healers needed now

your people new rings
their presence good news
summoning announcing
bad news now
good news for ever

Letter Thirty: **Violence**

Spirit of Peace,

Every day! Why every day? Can't the world catch a break, O Spirit of Peace?

There exist so many theories of why violence overcomes us. We debate endlessly "issues" relating to weapons of violence, weapons able to pierce bodies, hearts, spirits. The debate goes on, and children die, and the debate goes on, and even more succumb. Unborn and elderly become as one in a struggle for life. Entire populations seem secure in illusions of protection. Some governments spend inordinate sums on systems designed to "save."

Profits, prophets and motives get all mixed up in such scenarios. Prophetic exhortations jostle me, keeping me mindful of violence that leaves a heart bereft, aching to be cradled, not killed.

Spirit of Peace, hear my plea: Why don't we cherish the gift of life in a world that sometimes seems to run from you?

distant images
flash before me
mental download
neat and clean

continents away
visit my day
shattered bodies
my face-to-face view

nearer images of inside tremors
reveal haunting sprays of
gunfire familyfire
friendfire strangerfire

hearts seized and shaken
wail in disbelief:
O, Spirit of Peace,
when will madness end,
unmasking evil's surrender?

slowly, facing images begin the walk
lambs and lions
peeling away layers of resistance
momentary madness stripped of power
empowered embrace the lone assault
sisters and brothers free to be one in you

Letter Thirty-one: **Last One in the Door**

God of New Arrivals,

It was a long time coming, but I was still surprised. Others identified talents and gifts I had been too busy to notice, making this opportunity too good to pass up. So now I begin!

Yet I wonder, will longtime staff members support this "outsider"? What about the person who has labored for many years—perhaps a "prophet without honor"—just waiting for this opportunity, now missed?

Arrive with me, Spirit of God. Make of me a caring listener to colleagues on the watch for the last one in the door. Surface in me your gifts of wisdom and humility, for not even a new arrival knows it all.

welcome mat
spread wide
a new hero about to enter
ideas and solutions my companions now

hail!
the deliverer has arrived!

inner proclamations
sustain first days
my insights the balm
for others' malaise

but is this me?

your gift of perspective needed here
wisdom and humility
center stage
bearing a salute to services rendered
by service newly presented

curbside colleagues
and the new arrival
partners
fields of view mutually crafted
perspectives unlimited

hail!
deliverers side by side!

Letter Thirty-two: *False Judgment*

Just Judge,

I can't believe it! What is the source of such a judgment? How is it even possible that I could be judged in such a way?

In expressing my shock, I am surprised that my mind directs me to think about any judgments that may have fallen from my lips. After all, in today's world rash judgment seems a standard.

Perhaps, Lord, I need to purge my mind of thoughts similar to those motivating another to judge me unjustly. Hmmm... "But I *am* right," I tell myself.

What are you telling me, Lord?

neighbor serenity
engages me
friend integrity
commands my side

ethical living
always my calling card
shaken
in a millisecond

false judgment leaping forward
sensations of singular abandon
play tricks on me
doubt and bewilderment
spinning wildly within a wounded heart

with serenity shaken and integrity scarred
your arc of love encircles me
banners of justice and truth unfurled
in a testimony of innocence

gospel witnesses
of self-restoration
lead me on a new search
serenity integrity truth
the goal again

relief still needed
for another "so judged"

Letter Thirty-three: **Risk**

Spirit of New Discovery,

I sometimes look in an opposite direction, at least initially, when facing a risky situation. "All right, already, get on with it!" my inner voice bellows as I gingerly approach such moments. And suddenly I find myself ascertaining if I am facing a risk at all. Maybe this is just another slice of life with an unexpected turn.

Is my sense of risk related to some fear of unknown consequences that may follow a decision? To whom do I turn for support?

Spirit of God, some days I hear you in whispers that gently call to me, offering songs of confidence as I face new agendas. Thank you for people present in the whispers.

predictable ways
routine days
usual appeal,
assurances sealed

straight ahead life
no intrusion here
life to a human full:
reality or fear?

welcome risks
opportunities for tomorrows
change the straightaway

while hidden eyes speak my dilemma:
I don't want to and I do
still, I leap! I'm flying now!

my free fall question
what came over me?
no parachute amidst the whispers, the wind?

believe!

a new day before me
your presence, O Spirit of God,
in the feathered grasp of your people
your love in the whispers

Letter Thirty-four: **Poverty**

Spirit of the Lowly Ones,

First. First! I am to put poor and vulnerable people first? There are other firsts in my life, so I wonder sometimes about your call to especially attend to the needs of poor people.

Getting too close to this question could upset the way I've mapped out my life. For example, do I limit my attending to voices that cry out for justice, mercy and peace? Perhaps the truly graced are the deprived, the lowly, the ones whose hearts sing painful notes of suffering lives. They offer witness every moment of every day. How do I offer them hope, change?

Spirit of God, you know my vulnerabilities. You also know my gifts. Be with me as I claim poverty of spirit.

scenes and dreams
disrupt restless sleep
a wounded spirit
awakened to see

your defenseless
society's long forgotten
living the journey
as no others

pained heroic witnesses
struggling citizens of life
your weakened children
announcing a word of wisdom:

life is valued here
what is your first?
for whom do you thirst?

buts and priorities
prepackaged solutions
systems of sufficiency
offer little relief

gospel bearers summon my restless self
souls enlivened act as one
anguished spirits impoverished bodies
victorious
vulnerable children witnesses
every moment, every day

Letter Thirty-five: **Steps**

Lord of the Walk,

On Monday my steps are deliberate. By Wednesday I move with a little less bounce, but still progress. On Friday I step with caution, perhaps a sign of the week I've had. My steps are forward, backward, up, down, sideways. Some days I tiptoe, others I run. Some weeks all I seem to do is dance. Hah! These steps look spectacular, but take much more work.

Despite my changing daily movement, today's walk seems so similar to yesterday's. Will tomorrow's be any different? And if the daily walk is a bit routine, is that a limitation?

Jesus, the steps you took are traced and retraced by people of faith, scholars and curiosity seekers. When I make your steps my own, I am especially aware that you are walking with me. Then I realize it is you who gives me companions on the walk.

inching forward
a walker clings to a walker
one of metal
nearby, ones of flesh

a chaotic chase in a sea of sidewalks
from the starting gate an undetermined outcome
who will walk with the walker
stepping up to lend a step

my hope, stepping Lord,
is that another will say
I will help you walk today

I know, I know, my Lord,
why not me?
my preoccupied self begs for others
to help the walker move free

others converge
slower steps now the sign
I learn from the walker
it's really just time

your lesson for life
step back from this place
come join with the walkers
and steady your pace

Letter Thirty-six: **Anger**

Son of God,

"What? You did what? How could you say such a thing?"

The voice of anger reveals itself in many ways. It can be spoken by eyes of steel, a distant glance, a shout or the silent treatment. Techniques as numerous as there are people abound for expressing fury. I know that anger can be justified, but sometimes I wonder if it emerges more from habit than anything else.

Lord, guide my lips and my spirit when I sense anger surfacing. Help me to understand others' ire and reach out with a healing heart to help put anger aside.

swells of ire
too passionate verse
confirm limits reached
upsetting the peace

energies spent
too much to assess
yet the cost so severe
to relationships near

my spirit weakened,
anger's true yield
issues forth from exhaustion
and strained self-expression

wrath's plunder behind
day's end comes at last
the seeker's agenda
friends' counsel and life

your people the carriers
bearers of light
confront anger's woes
with wisdom tonight

such searchers and seekers
your guardians of peace
recover my spirit
through tired delight

Letter Thirty-seven: **Survival**

Eternal Protector,

What a great day! The bright sun cast a glistening sheen atop the lake's waters, a swimmer's delight. Today this swimmer would conquer a distant buoy, impressing my children with a father's glide through the water.

Without warning, a sharp pain ripped through me, forcing me under. Once, twice, three times I sank below the surface. Fear overcame me, even as a stranger grabbed hold of my writhing and waterlogged body, keeping me afloat until official rescuers pulled me ashore.

Now, years later, there are other moments "under the water." You are my rescuer, even—and especially—in the stranger. Lord, when am I the stranger, focused on others' survival?

clear thought slips away
panic the mode
survival instinct
my surface agenda

years pass not in days but seconds
birth life...death?
what claim is there for me?
what purpose in my demise?

salvation history
quite personal here
flailing movement
and frantic hope of new birth
rescuer's nightmare or dream?

still, I am saved

bleaker patterns
of breathless and wounded submersion
sometimes reappear, not just for me but for
sisters and brothers even deeper I see

and you are there

we sisters and brothers
survival's guests
strangers no more but rescuers together
in the flailing
in life's deep

Letter Thirty-eight: **Victim**

Christ with Us,

It's a day I'll never forget. Jostled and jolted, I felt like an acrobat as my contorted body stood on a crowded city bus. And suddenly I was violated. A trio of thieves exited rapidly as the bus slowed, my wallet in their possession. I was a victim.

Jesus, my first impression was one of emptiness, shock, surprise. How could this happen to me? Even worse, had I been targeted, followed? Now the pilferers had my address!

As I look back, I am a bit embarrassed to share my little anecdote in light of others' far more serious losses. But it's my experience.

I don't need to tell you what it's like to be a victim, Lord. Help me to be more attentive when colleagues, friends and family share with me the losses of their lives.

residual emptiness
memory of violation long ago
lives within
fading only with time

perhaps the present purpose
keen sense of mind
when before me I see
faces of others victimized

lamentations and losses too real to forget
limit depths and glances of forgiveness unmet

pain free of words
new eyes speak a message
words of the heart
encompassing me

saying no
to enforcers of resistance
your blessing of forgiving arms breaks forth
in the embrace
of memory and future

and we move from
mourning to morning
asking
who is the victim?

Letter Thirty-nine: **Reflection**

God of My Reflection,

It doesn't crack! I look in the mirror, set a wild and uncontrollable hair in place and do a quick self-study for the "right look." In my haste to leave on time, the mirror seems to look back at me (with hair in place!).

Reflections. Is what I see, Lord, what others see? Most days the "me in the mirror" appears to be crisper, on top of things, eager to launch into the day's agenda. Realistically, though, the "me who leaves" goes through the day facing other faces, challenges, twists and turns. All the while, my mirrored self basks in the security of the sheltered self.

Lord, you enliven me as I ponder your gift of life. May my life reflect with deep joy the wonder of being made in your image and likeness.

pools and streams of clarity
enable
soft reflections to look back at me
your view through facial form
into the depths of my soul

you know, O Lord, the self
you see what lies within
offering companions
to take your gift inside

along the way
passing scarred moments
long forgotten memories
high points and low

mystery and wonder of life
magnificence
in moments and movements
of the unstifled journey within

gladness my home
mercy my resting place
self-disclosure my door
to enduring love

reflections of your people
beside me
tender images of graced life

Letter Forty: **Belonging**

Lord of Nearness,

We are people who long to belong. We gather naturally. So it must seem odd that from within belonging can come woundedness.

At one point in my life, I went from a great sense of being out of place with one group to a deep sense of belonging with another. The change was dramatic, especially in the way I perceived reality. And the pain when something went wrong in the new group was, not surprisingly, severe. I saw that there can be a cost to belonging.

Lord, you have borne the cost of belonging. It is you to whom we belong. I long for you, O God. Be ever near.

in a retinue of risings and retirings
I long
long for you

your counsel my treasure
for gathering
with brothers and sisters
in a common chant of angelic blend

the language?
of love, of life without end

humility rejoicing
your people reborn belonging in you
daybreak witness
of faithfulness always, disciples' delight

O Lord, belonging's messengers
lend spirited solemnity
with praise thanks and glory
for love always near

in love's sanctuary
you dwell deep within
with a love so lasting
it is never to end

O Lord, be not far
we long
long for you